KV-512-212

TABLE OF CONTENTS

INTRODUCTION

In writing this book, I hope to demonstrate the many different approaches to playing jazz saxophone. By including a biography, selected discography, and a brief style analysis on each player, I wish to place them all in their historic context. Included are some of the finest and most influential tenor sax players, each with his own unique style.

Prior to Coleman Hawkins, the saxophone was used predominantly for comedic relief in Vaudeville shows. Hawkins saw the instrument's true possibilities and "rescued" the saxophone by solidifying its role in jazz. From then on, the innovations have continued: from the early-1930's swing style of Hawkins and Lester Young, to the bebop-inspired solos of Harold Land and Sonny Stitt, to the more modern 1960s sounds of John Coltrane and Sonny Rollins, the musical possibilities of the saxophone are endless, limited only by the artist's imagination and skill.

But skill and imagination need something to build upon—a foundation. The Louvre in Paris has a long tradition of encouraging visual artists to copy from the masters; thousands have done so, including several of the greats: Manet, Degas, Chagall, and even Dali and Picasso. The idea is that if you don't copy, you can't advance—use the masterworks as a point of departure. Don't just copy passively, but let the great players of yesterday inspire you to create something that is more than a reproduction—something that is your own. To that end, I've quoted some of each player's favorite licks as a launching point. On the CD, I play the solos in the style of each player, the goal being to capture some of the aspects that helped to define their unique voices—the essence of each player's style. Mastering these solos will help you to improvise in a wide variety of styles.

I strongly encourage you to pick up the original recordings of these artists and listen to them firsthand. The Selected Discography at the end of each chapter lists some of the quintessential recordings of each player's career. The ultimate goal, of course, is to develop one's own voice. It's the unique combination of influences and the individual tone quality as well as personality that makes each of these artists unique.

Pianist Walter Bishop, Jr. once said, "It all goes from imitation to assimilation to innovation. You move from the imitation stage to the assimilation stage when you take little bits of things from different people and weld them into an identifiable style—creating your own style. Once you've created your own sound and you have a good sense of the history of the music, then you think of where the music hasn't gone and where it can go—and that's innovation."[1] Have fun...

—*Dennis Taylor*

---

[1] from *Thinking in Jazz: The Infinite Art of Improvisation* by Paul F. Berliner (University of Chicago Press, 1994)

CD INCLUDES **16 FULL-BAND** TRACKS

JAZZ SAXOPHONE

An In-Depth Look at the Styles of the Tenor Masters

By Dennis Taylor

LESSONS

MUSIC

HISTORICAL ANALYSIS

RARE PHOTOS

Cover photos provided by the
Frank Driggs Collection.
Clockwise from lower left: Sonny Rollins,
Lester Young, Dexter Gordon,
John Coltrane, Stan Getz.

ISBN 0-634-05849-5

HAL•LEONARD®
CORPORATION
7777 W. BLUEMOUND RD. P.O. BOX 13819 MILWAUKEE, WI 53213

Visit Hal Leonard Online at
www.halleonard.com

ACKNOWLEDGMENTS

Special thanks go to my wife Karen for her constant support, encouragement, and editing talents, and to my parents Ad & Lois for instilling in me the love of music and the belief that anything is possible.

THE RECORDING

On the accompanying CD, the sax tracks can be removed by turning the balance knob all the way to the right, allowing you to play the written solo (or your own) along with the band. Follow the track numbers (🔊) at the beginning of each written music example to find your place on the CD.

Musicians:

Darryl Dybka – piano

John Vogt – bass

Chris Brown – drums

Dennis Taylor – tenor saxophone

Recorded at Tone Chaparral, Nashville, Tennessee

Engineered and mixed by George Bradfute

LESTER YOUNG ("PREZ")

(1909 – 1959)

L ester Young broke all the rules—not only for tenor saxophone, but for all of jazz. Young became one of the genre's most original and creative practitioners.

Born in Mississippi and raised in Algiers, LA, Young was taught drums, trumpet, alto sax, and violin by his father and spent most of his youth drumming in the Young Family Band. By his late teens, he had given up the drums and switched to alto sax. (He noticed that all the young women had left the gig by the time he finished packing up his drum kit.) He joined Art Bronson's Bostonians as a tenor sax player from 1928–29, then freelanced for a few years with Bennie Moten, King Oliver, and had a brief stint with the Count Basie Orchestra. In 1934 he joined Fletcher Henderson's Orchestra to fill Coleman Hawkins's vacated chair.

Frank Driggs Collection

A giant of jazz saxophone, Lester Young led the way from swing to bebop to cool jazz.

Young's light, airy tone and linear approach were too foreign to Henderson's sidemen. Henderson's wife would take Young into their basement and make him study Hawkins's recorded solos to learn how to play "correctly." Although Henderson was pleased with his playing, the mocking of the other sidemen led Young to leave the band after just a few months. In 1936 he rejoined the Basie Orchestra, and was with the band when it relocated to New York City. There he made his recording debut on a John Hammond-produced four-song session with a small version of Basie's band. Two of those songs, "Lady Be Good" and "Shoe Shine Boy," made a revolutionary impact, challenging the reign of Coleman Hawkins as the top sax soloist.

Young's mellow sound and hard-swinging solos were a perfect fit with the Basie Orchestra. Soon he was the featured soloist and a major attraction for the band. For the next four years he played on all of the Count's recording dates, as well as some of Billie Holliday's finest recordings. His light touch and gravity-free style of playing were a perfect blend with Holliday, who proclaimed him the "President of the Saxophone" (shortened to "Prez"); he affectionately dubbed her "Lady Day."

In 1940, Prez left the Basie Orchestra to co-lead a band with his brother, drummer Lee Young, and he also worked with Al Sears's Big Band for a while. In 1943 he returned to the Basie Orchestra, but a recording strike kept the band from making any records during this period (a few air checks are all that have been preserved). In 1944 Young was drafted, and shortly after his induction he was sentenced to a prison term at a detention barracks in Georgia due to his admission on a routine form that he smoked pot. There he was said to have been beaten and abused. After his discharge in 1945, he resumed his recording with the tune "DB Blues" (DB = "Detention Barracks"). The youthful exuberance in his playing was gone, but a more revealing and vulnerable quality appeared. Young made some of his finest recordings during the latter half of the forties, maintaining his spot in the hierarchy of jazz soloists despite the advent of bebop. Throughout the fifties, he led his own combo and had a few reunions with Basie. Always a loner, Young became increasingly retiring and distrusting. His health got progressively worse due to alcoholism, and in March of 1959 he died in his New York City hotel room just hours after returning from an engagement in Paris.

Musically Speaking:

Lester Young was profoundly original—from his dress, to his own invented language, to his way of holding his sax off-center at a rakish angle. His revolutionary tone was modeled after C-melody saxophonist Frankie Trumbauer and altoist Jimmy Dorsey, yielding a lighter tone with slower vibrato. This style—which would later give birth to the "cool" movement in jazz—gives the impression of poise and control rather than effort and abandon.

Young's style of improvisation is based on the horizontal melodic line—a method of focusing on the melody's forward motion by using scales. He restricted himself to playing in key centers by finding a scale that would fit over a series of chords. In doing so, he would often find himself playing the "pretty" notes—those found on the upper extensions of the chord, like the 9th, 11th, and 13th. When Young did play an arpeggio, he chose one that would fit over several chords (as in meas. A9, A10, and A30—the notes E, C#, and A are used over A major, D7, and E7 chords). This approach allowed him considerable latitude in constructing his lines, enabling him to stress the lyrical content of his solos.

Young's approach to rhythm was equally innovative. His phrases were asymmetrical, breaking through the four- and eight-measure tradition of his predecessors. Young would lay out over beats that other players would accent; he would end phrases unexpectedly and turn clichés inside out, making his solos exciting and unpredictable. Syncopation (meas. A4–6), cross-rhythms (B9–11; B26–28), and glissandos (B21) dominated Young's lines, adding to his sense of soaring over the rhythm section.

TRACK 1

Lester Young Selected Discography

1936–39	*Essential Count Basie, Vol. 1 & 2* – Columbia Jazz Master
1946	*Complete Lester Young on Keynote* – (with Nat King Cole & Buddy Rich) – Verve
1956	*Lester Young with the Oscar Peterson Trio* – Verve
1994	*Lester Young Jazz Masters 30: 1943-1952* – Verve
1997	*The Kansas City Sessions, 1938-1944* – GRP

*Coleman Hawkins is the father of jazz saxophone. A pioneer, he's credited with developing
the role of saxophone in jazz, becoming the instrument's first premier jazz soloist.*

COLEMAN HAWKINS ("HAWK")

(1904–1969)

At the 1963 Newport Jazz Festival, vocalist Jon Hendricks introduced Coleman Hawkins as "the man for whom Adolphe Sax invented the saxophone." Hawk's long career (over half a century) is one of the most brilliant chapters in jazz history. A pioneer who rescued the saxophone from a life of comedic relief in vaudeville, he created a medium for jazz sax. An inspired soloist, he made major contributions to the development of jazz as an art form. As an established star, he was the bridge between the swing and bebop eras.

Born in St. Louis, MO, Coleman Hawkins began his musical training with piano at age 5, cello at age 7, then saxophone two years later. At Washburn College in Topeka, KS, he acquired a foundation in music theory that would become the building block of his playing style. He left college before graduating, toured and recorded with Mamie Smith's Jazz Hounds, and eventually settled in New York City. In 1923 he joined Fletcher Henderson's band, and for the next decade was their featured sax soloist. In 1924, Louis Armstrong joined the Henderson band and became a big influence on Hawk's style.

In the spring of 1934, Hawkins left Henderson to tour England and France with British big-band leader Jack Hylton, only to leave the band when he wasn't allowed into Germany because of his race. For the next four years he toured Western Europe, doing pickup gigs and working with his own small groups. He was treated as a great artist and contributed greatly to the growing popularity of jazz on the continent. Upon returning to the U.S. in 1939, he found many young tenor players ready to duel for his crown. Hawk had built a reputation for doing "battle" in jam sessions and, as legend has it, only Lester Young was ever able to beat him in a cutting session. (Both giants on the instrument, their styles were so dissimilar that these "battles" merely demonstrated the limitless possibilities of jazz.)

In October of 1939, Hawkins recorded his masterpiece, "Body and Soul," one of the most famous jazz recordings of all time. As the story goes, late in the session the producer convinced a reluctant Hawkins to record the song. A couple measures into it, he abandoned the melody for two choruses, playing a tight-knit improvised sonata featuring his cascading arpeggios infused with subtle chord substitutions and a steady rhythmic pulse. Always an innovator, in 1944 Hawk led a band for the record date that was to become the first bebop session. Included on that date were Dizzy Gillespie, Oscar Pettiford, and Max Roach. While many of his contemporaries dismissed this new radical music (Armstrong called it "Chinese Music"), Hawkins embraced it and adapted his style to the new modernists, hiring young bebop players such as Thelonious Monk, Miles Davis, and Howard McGee for his various bands. Also in 1944, Hawkins began a long intermittent association with Norman Granz's *Jazz at the Philharmonic* tours.

Late in his career, he continued to stand toe-to-toe with the best sax players of the time. In 1957 he was sideman on a Monk date that paired him with John Coltrane; in 1963 he recorded with Sonny Rollins. Cannonball Adderly liked to tell of a young sax player who grumbled to him that Coleman Hawkins made him nervous. Adderly replied, "Hawkins is supposed to make you nervous. Hawkins has been making other sax players nervous for forty years."

Musically speaking:

During Coleman Hawkins's long career as patriarch of the saxophone, he continued to search for new and meaningful ways to express himself. His early solos with Fletcher Henderson in the mid-1920s featured a clown-like tongue-slapping effect. From Louis Armstrong he developed long flowing lines and lyricism. His phrasing was almost baroque in approach; his music was filled with ornamentation and decoration, swinging, arpeggiated lines, delineating the chords in a vertical approach, and often linking the chords with his own distinctive chord substitutions. Switching from swing to bebop, Hawkins altered his phrasing and harmonies to fit the new music. He had a huge, husky tone (transferring the sonorities of the cello to the sax), a thick vibrato, and an occasional growl with facile technique.

The following solo shows Hawkins's thematic development, tremendous driving pulse, and vertical outlines of harmonies. His playing directly influenced Ben Webster, John Coltrane, Sonny Rollins, and essentially anyone who ever picked up the sax after him. Hawkins dominated five decades of jazz, creating a language for the saxophone and the development of jazz as an art form.

Coleman Hawkins Selected Discography

1936-1965　　*Body & Soul* – (Compilation) RCA

1943　　*Classic Tenors: Lester Young & Coleman Hawkins* – Flying Dutchman

1944　　*Rainbow Mist* – Delmark

1957　　*Coleman Hawkins Encounters Ben Webster* – Verve

1957　　*The Hawk Flies High* – Original Jazz Classics

1962　　*Duke Ellington meets Coleman Hawkins* – Impulse!

1965　　*Wrapped Tight* – Impulse!

Frank Driggs Collection

Ben Webster, seen here playing Ol' Betsy, a 1938 Selmer Balanced Action Tenor
(the only sax he played his entire career), was one of the founding fathers of swing saxophone.

BEN WEBSTER

(1909 – 1973)

Ben Webster's swinging style makes him the link between Coleman Hawkins and Lester Young. The three are considered the tenor triumvirate—the founding fathers of the 1930s-style tenor jazz saxophone.

Webster started on violin as a child in Kansas City, MO. He switched to piano and was schooled in blues by his neighbor, boogie-woogie great Pete Johnson. Webster played piano in a few territory bands but mainly worked as a soloist. While playing for silent movies at a theater in Amarillo, TX, he met sax player Budd Johnson, who introduced him to the fundamentals of the instrument. Shortly thereafter, Webster was invited by Lester Young's father, Willis, to join the saxophone section of the Young Family Band. Willis Young tutored Webster in reading music and furthered his study of sax technique. From there, Webster joined Bennie Moten's orchestra and became a featured soloist on some of Moten's landmark recordings. After touring with some of the best orchestras in the thirties (the big bands of Andy Kirk, Fletcher Henderson, Benny Carter, Willie Bryant, Cab Calloway, and the short-lived Teddy Wilson Big Band), Webster joined the Duke Ellington Orchestra on a permanent basis in 1940, becoming their first featured tenor soloist. Ellington expanded the sax section to five to accommodate Webster, who took part in many of the Orchestra's classic recordings and was featured on "Cottontail," "Chelsea Bridge," and "All Too Soon."

The renown Webster achieved with Ellington led him to strike out on his own. He recorded frequently as a leader and sideman (and returned to Ellington for a quick tour of duty in 1948-49). Settling in New York City, he worked the clubs on 52nd Street regularly and toured with Norman Granz's *Jazz at the Philharmonic*. By the early fifties, Webster moved back to Kansas City, then to L.A. to be near his ailing mother. He recorded with Art Tatum, Coleman Hawkins, Billie Holliday, Oscar Peterson, and a host of others.

By the mid-sixties, Webster's sound and style of playing had slipped out of fashion. With few prospects in the U.S., Webster moved to Amsterdam in 1965, then to Copenhagen in 1969, where he was based until his death in 1973.

Musically speaking:

Jazz writer Whitney Balliett described Webster's tone as "a wonder of music... perhaps the broadest ever achieved on the instrument." Webster's thirties swing style was initially influenced by Benny Carter and Webster's idol, Coleman Hawkins. He had a gruff, raspy tone on the swing numbers, yet on ballads he would play in an intimate, warm tone with tender emotion and thick vibrato—starting at a whisper, exploding into a full tone, then melting back down to a sub-tone (more air than a distinct pitch). While in Ellington's band, Webster came under the influence of his section-mate, alto saxophonist Johnny Hodges, who taught him about the seductive qualities of tone, emotion, and lyricism. Hodges' influence is readily heard in Webster's upper-register playing.

Webster was at his best at slow and medium tempos; the following solo illustrates his medium swing style. His phrasing was short and concise, based on quarter- and eighth-note rhythms with flowery ornamentation and punctuated by his distinctive growl. His playing influenced many saxophonists including Charlie Rouse, Eddie "Lockjaw" Davis, Paul Gonsalves, Gerry Mulligan, Bennie Wallace, and Scott Hamilton. Webster played his Selmer Balanced Action tenor, bought in 1938 (dubbed "Ol' Betsy"), for his entire career, leaving specific instructions that upon his death, his sax was never to be played again. It now rests in the Institute of Jazz Studies at Rutgers University.

Ben Webster Selected Discography

1985   *The Big Tenor: The Complete Ben Webster on EmArcy* – (1951-1953) – EmArcy

1957   *Soulville* – Verve

1959   *Ben Webster meets Gerry Mulligan* – Verve

1959   *Ben Webster meets Oscar Peterson* – Verve

1964   *Meet You at the Fair* – Impulse!

1965   *Stormy Weather* – Black Lion

Frank Driggs Collection

Paul Gonsalves is best known for his crowd-pleasing twenty-seven chorus romp in the tune "Diminuendo and Crescendo in Blue" at the 1956 Newport Jazz Festival.

PAUL GONSALVES

(1920 – 1974)

Duke Ellington described Paul Gonsalves as "a wonderful musician, highly skilled with tremendous imagination. He is equipped to perform whatever comes to his mind."

The son of Cape Verde natives, Paul Gonsalves was raised in Providence, RI. His father taught him and his two brothers to play Portuguese folk dances on the guitar. Paul's oldest brother, Joe, turned him on to jazz, listening to the big bands of the day: Ellington, Henderson, and Lunceford. Paul picked up the sax after attending a Jimmy Lunceford concert, and he gigged in New England until he joined the army in 1942. He settled in Boston after his discharge, then joined the Basie band from 1946–49. That was followed by two years (1949–50) with Dizzy Gillespie. He joined Duke Ellington's band in 1950 and, except for a brief stint with Tommy Dorsey's band in 1953, stayed with the Ellington orchestra until his death twenty-four years later.

The early fifties saw the rise of bebop in jazz and R&B in popular music, and Duke Ellington was struggling to keep his big band afloat. A spectacular performance at Newport in 1956, thanks in large part to Gonsalves's stomping, crowd-pleasing twenty-seven-chorus solo in the composition "Diminuendo and Crescendo in Blue," righted the ship and put Ellington on the cover of *Time* magazine. This performance, recorded for the album *Ellington At Newport*, was intended to be a comeback of sorts. On a hunch, Ellington called a seldom-played chart, instructing Gonsalves to just "go as long as you want" during the interlude. The Gonsalves solo was one of the longest and most unusual ever recorded. After the first third of his solo, the audience was on its feet, cheering and clapping and egging him on. Gonsalves dug in and swung even harder, going chorus after chorus and sending the concertgoers into a complete frenzy. He began each chorus with a riff, then built on that riff to create tension and momentum, each chorus building upon the next. The solo was pure hard-driving swing at its finest, without the histrionics of honking low notes and high squeals. From then on, Gonsalves was obliged to play an extended uptempo solo each performance, overshadowing his relaxed and thoughtful ballad playing.

Ellington always credited Gonsalves with helping to revive his career, and the lives and careers of the two were intertwined for the rest of their days. When Gonsalves died in London in 1974, Ellington was too ill to be told. Ellington himself died a few days later.

Musically Speaking:

Paul Gonsalves was influenced by Coleman Hawkins and Ben Webster. "Coleman Hawkins is my main influence. There was something in his music that coincided with Duke's, that for me denoted class."[2]

Gonsalves was harmonically advanced, thanks in part to his early training on guitar. He was able to build momentum by playing tension notes that needed to be resolved. (The listener's ear wants to hear the resolutions, as in measures A31–B5 and C12–C15 of the following example.) His well of musical ideas ran deep; he rarely repeated himself. Gonsalves's distinctive way of playing over the chords gave his dramatic improvisations a completely unique voice filled with passion and wit, a smoky sound spiced with swing and blues licks.

---

[2] from *The World Of Duke Ellington* by Stanley Dance.

Paul Gonsalves Selected Discography

1961   *Gettin' Together* – Riverside

1963   *Tell It the Way It Is* – Impulse

1964   *Salt and Pepper* (with Sonny Stitt) – Impulse

with Duke Ellington:

1956   Ellington at Newport – Columbia

1966   Far East Suite – Bluebird

1967   And His Mother Called Him Bill – RCA

Gene Ammons' style combined the harmonic concepts of bebop with the soulfulness of the blues.

GENE AMMONS ("JUG")

(1925 – 1974)

Son of boogie-woogie piano player Albert Ammons, Gene Ammons blended R&B, blues, and bebop.

Gene Ammons was raised in Chicago. At the age of eighteen he joined trumpeter King Kolax's blues band. Ammons first came into national prominence when he joined Billy Eckstine's seminal big band (1944–47), in which he was used primarily as the bebop-style soloist. He was featured on the "tenor battle" with Dexter Gordon on Eckstine's record *Blowing the Blues Away*.

When Eckstine's band disbanded, Ammons stepped into the spotlight to form his own combo, playing blues-infused jazz. His version of "My Foolish Heart" was the first release on the fledgling Chess Records in 1950. That same year, Ammons formed his famous alliance with saxophonist Sonny Stitt and recorded the two-tenor classic "Blues Up and Down." The duo toured and recorded together for two years before going off to front their own bands. Ammons had several jukebox hits including "Canadian Sunset," "Ca 'Purange," and "Didn't We."

Ammons's drug problems led to two jail sentences—from 1958–60 and 1962–69. After the second sentence, his playing style changed a bit; he began incorporating some of the "frenzied" avant-garde style of playing that was in vogue at the time, but retained a funky rhythm section. Ammons continued to lead his own organ combos and soul/jazz groups until his death in 1974.

Musically Speaking:

Gene Ammons distilled equal parts of Coleman Hawkins and Lester Young into his own distinct voice. His thick, resonant tone and firm attack owed much to Hawkins, while his rhythmic sense and blues accents recalled Young. Ammons played with relaxed, laid-back phrasing with sudden staccato bursts of double-time. He had an especially emotive ballad style: very lyrical, soulful, and leisurely—he never went double-time on the ballads. Ammons's harmonic conception reflected the modernism and sophistication of bebop with the soulful, gritty edge of the blues.

Gene Ammons had a great influence on the world of R&B and jazz, influencing (among others) Stanley Turrentine, A.C. Reed, and Houston Person.

Gene Ammons Selected Discography

1950   *Blues Up and Down, Vol. 1* – Prestige

1958   *Blue Gene* – Original Jazz Classics

1960   *Boss Tenor* – Prestige

1960   *Gene Ammons Story: Organ Combo* – Prestige

1961   *Boss Tenors* (with Sonny Stitt) – PolyGram

DEXTER GORDON ("LTD")

(1923 – 1990)

Dexter Gordon ("Long Tall Dexter") was one of the first to translate Charlie Parker's bebop style from alto to tenor saxophone. He was raised in Los Angeles, CA, the son of a doctor/jazz aficionado whose patients included Duke Ellington and Lionel Hampton. Gordon picked up the clarinet at age 13, switching first to alto saxophone and then to tenor sax two years later.

Dexter Gordon was one of the first to translate Charlie Parker's bebop style to the tenor sax.

The L.A. of Gordon's youth enjoyed a thriving jazz scene. As a teenager he studied music with Lloyd Reese and played in a rehearsal band that included Charlie Mingus and Buddy Collette. At age seventeen he joined the Lionel Hampton big band and came under the tutelage of the principal tenor soloist, Illinois Jacquet. His playing style, which had been reminiscent of Lester Young, adopted a more hard-edged sound and aggressive style. Gordon made his recording debut as a leader in 1943, on a date that included Nat King Cole on piano. In 1943–44 he toured briefly with Lee Young (brother of Lester Young), Fletcher Henderson, and Louis Armstrong.

Gordon moved to New York City in 1944 to join Billy Eckstine's seminal bebop big band, supplementing a sax section that already included Sonny Stitt on alto and Gene Ammons on tenor. The two tenors were featured on "Blowing the Blues Away." Gordon often jammed with Charlie Parker at late-night jam sessions. After 1946, Gordon lived a bi-coastal lifestyle, working with Tad Dameron in NYC and teaming up with fellow saxophonist Wardell Gray in L.A. The two locked horns in some epic tenor battles during the forties and fifties, the most famous being "The Chase," which became Dial's largest-selling record. Gray's relaxed style served as the perfect contrast to Gordon's full-toned aggressive approach.

The fifties were lean years for Gordon. A 1952 heroin bust landed him in jail for two years. The advent of "cool jazz," then in vogue in L.A., left Gordon's hard-driving bop style in little demand. In 1959 he was asked to lead a jazz quartet, compose the music, and act in the L.A. production of the Jack Gelber play *The Connection*. This led to his appearance in the critically acclaimed 1961 movie adaptation, *The Hollywood Connection*.

In 1960, Cannonball Adderly produced Gordon's first recording in five years, *Resurgence* (Riverside Records). In 1961, Gordon returned to NYC and signed with Blue Note Records. From 1961–65 he recorded four titles for the label, containing some of his finest playing. During that same period, he guested on a Herbie Hancock date that included "Watermelon Man," a song that would become a jazz classic. On his 1962 trip to London and the Continent, Gordon fell in love with the European lifestyle and took up residence first in Paris, then in Copenhagen for the next fifteen years. During this period he performed at many of the European Jazz Festivals, taught courses and master classes, and continued to record—including a series of live albums at Copenhagen's famed Montmartre Club.

In 1976, Gordon returned to NYC for a two-night engagement at the Storyville Club. The ovation he received stunned him—he had to plead exhaustion at 3 a.m. to avoid another encore. The second night, Columbia Records' Bruce Lundvall offered to sign him on the spot. The tremendous demand for Gordon resulted in a weeklong stay at the Village Vanguard, where crowds stretched out into the street. The proceedings were recorded and became the two-album set *Homecoming*, one of the landmark jazz recordings of the seventies. Gordon remained in the U.S. and continued to tour and record with his own band until his death in 1990. His powerful performance in the 1986 film *Round Midnight* earned him an Oscar nomination.

Musically Speaking:

Dexter Gordon combined Lester Young's lyricism and laid-back phrasing with the bebop rhythms of Charlie Parker and the huge tone of Coleman Hawkins. He sometimes lagged so far behind the beat that it seemed impossible for him to catch up. Gordon said that "Hawkins was going out farther on the chords, but Lester leaned on the pretty notes. He had a way of telling a story with everything he played." His ballad playing, deeply rooted in the classic thirties and forties sound of Hawkins and Webster, exposed his sentimental side. Humor was also a large element of Gordon's style—he often quoted snippets from other songs as a kind of musical inside joke.

Dexter Gordon Selected Discography

1951   *Dexter Calling* – Blue Note

1961   *Doin' Alright* – Blue Note

1963   *Our Man in Paris* – Blue Note

1964   *One Flight Up* – Blue Note

1964   *Cheesecake* – Steeplechase

1976   *Homecoming: Live at the Village Vanguard* – Columbia

ZOOT SIMS

(1925 – 1985)

John Haley "Zoot" Sims was an eloquent, hard-swinging tenor sax soloist in the style of Lester Young. He cut his musical teeth in the famed big bands of his day, but preferred the freedom of the small combo setting.

California-born Sims grew up in a Vaudeville family. He started out playing clarinet and drums, then moved to tenor sax at age 13. Sims dropped out of high school at age fourteen and started touring on the dance band circuit. He joined Benny Goodman's Orchestra in 1943 for the first of many collaborations. Sims was one of Goodman's favorite tenor players, and they worked together intermittently over the next forty years.

Sims made his recording debut in 1944 with pianist Joe Bushkin. He rejoined Benny Goodman in 1946–47. From 1947–49, Sims was a member of Woody Herman's band, The Second Herd, and gained attention as a member of Herman's famed sax section: Sims, Stan Getz, Herbie Steward, and Serge Chaloff (a.k.a. "the Four Brothers," named for the Jimmy Guiffre composition). In 1953, Sims recorded and

© Lee Tanner

Zoot Sims was a master of phrasing, playing long, clean, floating lines in the style of Lester Young.

toured with Stan Kenton. He was then a featured soloist in the Gerry Mulligan Concert Jazz Band from 1954–56. While in Mulligan's band, he formed a lasting musical bond with fellow tenor player Al Cohn, with whom he shared a similar style and approach. Much of the remainder of Sims's career was spent leading his own combo or co-leading with Cohn. He also toured frequently as a member of Norman Granz's *Jazz at the Philharmonic* tours. A much sought-after collaborator, Sims also recorded with Joe Pass, Count Basie, Harry "Sweets" Edison, and Jimmy Rowles.

Musically speaking:

Sims was a very consistent player, generating great momentum with his clean, logical, floating lines. He played with a light tone à la "Prez," though over time his tone gained depth and his playing became more reminiscent of Ben Webster—especially on the ballads. Sims was masterful at phrasing and re-phrasing an idea. His phrases were constantly moving, dancing over the bar lines. In his own words, "There's one thing I've never lost yet, that I remember having when I was young: a feeling that tomorrow I'm going to play better, or I think I'm going to play better than I did today." Art Pepper, Scott Hamilton, and Harry Allen are among the sax players influenced by Sims.

Zoot Sims Selected Discography

1948   *The Second Herd 1948* (with Woody Herman) – Storyville

1956   *Zoot!* – Original Jazz Classics

1978   *For Lady Day* – Pablo

1978   *Just Friends* – Original Jazz Classics

1983   *Blues for Two* – Pablo

*Sonny Stitt's playing was driven by a forceful rhythmic sense,
precise articulation, and blazing technique.*

SONNY STITT

(1924 – 1982)

Sonny Stitt was a fiery bebop soloist on both tenor and alto. Born Edward Stitt in Boston, he grew up in Saginaw, MI surrounded by music—his father was a music teacher, his mother played piano and organ, and his brother Clifford was a concert pianist. At age seven, Sonny started playing piano, later switching to clarinet and then alto sax. His early influences were Johnny Hodges and Benny Carter.

Stitt made his recording debut with Tiny Bradshaw in the early 1940s. He joined Billy Eckstine's revolutionary bebop-based big band in 1945, in a sax section that also included Dexter Gordon and Gene Ammons. In this setting, Stitt found a musical situation conducive to his advanced style of playing. 1946 found him working on and off with Eckstine, and he was also a member of the first short-lived Dizzy Gillespie Big Band; he recorded with Gillespie in May of that year.

After a prison term for a drug bust, Stitt moved to New York City in 1949 to find bebop waning and Miles Davis already "blowing cool." Stitt was growing tired of always being cast in the Charlie Parker mold, and he found that by switching to tenor he could distance himself from comparisons to "Bird." (He didn't go back to the alto until after Parker's death in 1955.) His sound on tenor became markedly more individual—influenced by Lester Young, Don Byas, and his old bandmate Dexter Gordon. Stitt's first recording on tenor was for trombonist J.J. Johnson's session in 1949; he then did several albums with his own combo for Prestige, Argo, and Verve during the fifties. For a brief period in 1960, Stitt joined Miles Davis, replacing John Coltrane. That was short-lived, however; Miles felt that Stitt's solos were too bebop-based for his modal excursions of the time. After Miles, Stitt played and recorded with many organ combos, including those of Don Patterson and Brother Jack McDuff. He also co-led a group with Gene Ammons for some classic two-tenor "battles."

In 1971, Stitt joined the all-star aggregation "Giants of Jazz," a band that included Dizzy Gillespie, Thelonious Monk, Kai Winding, Art Blakey, and Al McKibbon. He continued to play and record up until his death in 1982.

Musically speaking:

Sonny Stitt's playing was driven by a forceful rhythmic sense, precise articulation, and blazing technique. Everything he played had a touch of bebop in it. His switch from alto to tenor gave him a more distinctive sound; on tenor he still had the fleet-fingered aggressiveness, but his ideas were more concise.

Stitt's playing is characterized by a syncopated sense of rhythm, melodies made up primarily of eighth notes, chromatic approaches to chord tones, and chords with altered 5ths and 9ths. He possessed a large arsenal of pet licks, patterns, melodic lines, and chord substitutions that he would weave in and out in a very compelling manner. With his reedy tone and light touch, Stitt's music was always strong, immediate, and explosive.

In the following example, liberal chord alterations are arrived at by chromatic approaches to chord tones and altering the 9ths and 5ths. Section D is another favorite device of Stitt's: a long outro vamp at the end of a song (in this case, a repeated four-measure pattern: I–VI7–IIm7–V7). Stitt was a master at sequencing his phrases, as in measures A1–2, D5–8, and D13–D16.

Sonny Stitt Selected Discography

1949   *Sonny Stitt with Bud Powell and J.J. Johnson* – Prestige

1961   *Boss Tenors* (with Gene Ammons) – Verve

1995   *Stitt Meets Brother Jack* (with Jack McDuff) – Prestige

1963   *Stitt Plays Bird* – Atlantic

1972   *Tune-Up* – Muse

1998   *Soul Classics 1962-1972* (Reissue compilation) – Prestige

© Lee Tanner

An uncompromising, brilliant soloist, continually reinventing himself,
Sonny Rollins is one of jazz's all-time great improvisers.

SONNY ROLLINS
(1930 –)

One of the all-time greatest tenor saxophonists, Sonny Rollins has been a commanding presence since the 1950s. With his huge, edgy, resonant tone, speech-like phrasing, harmonic approach, and thematic style of improvisation, Rollins defies categorization.

Sonny Rollins grew up in the Sugar Hill section of Harlem, NY. He began studying music on piano and switched to sax by age 11. Coleman Hawkins lived in his neighborhood and was an early influence. At age nineteen, Rollins made his recording debut with singer Babs Gonzales. For the next six years he recorded as a sideman with such jazz luminaries as J.J. Johnson, Bud Powell, Thelonious Monk, and Miles Davis, who paired him up with a tenor-playing Charlie Parker in 1955. Rollins's reputation grew from his outstanding work in the Clifford Brown/Max Roach quintet. When that group disbanded due to Brown's untimely death, Rollins headed out on his own.

Rollins's early recordings displayed a talented player in the style of Dexter Gordon—combining the robust tone of Coleman Hawkins (sans vibrato) with the rhythmic and asymmetrical phrasing of Lester Young. By 1956, Rollins had discovered his own voice and released his landmark recording, *Saxophone Colossus*. In 1957, he recorded the album *Way Out West* with just bass and drums, eliminating the piano—an idea with which he had experimented before, but not for an entire recording. This allowed him to play fragments of themes in even more harmonic variations, without being boxed in by a chordal instrument. Still using the trio format in 1958, Rollins released *Freedom Suite*, on which he addressed racial and artistic freedom.

In 1959 Rollins, not yet thirty, took the first of his self-imposed sabbaticals. He used this time to reinvent himself, spending many nights practicing on NYC's Williamsburg Bridge. He developed a new tone—warmer and huskier—and formulated his "system of orchestration," a new way of arranging his thematic approach. After a two-year break he returned to the studio, signing a lucrative contract to record six albums for RCA; the first of these is called (naturally) *The Bridge*. All six were masterful and groundbreaking, covering the spectrum of jazz from hard bop to Latin, and even including a foray into Ornette Coleman-inspired free jazz. In 1967, Rollins again went into exile and did not enter a studio for five years. When he returned he had reinvented himself again, using a more pentatonic-modal approach with a broader, edgier tone.

Sonny Rollins leaves an unparalleled legacy of monumental improvisations and compositions. His tunes "Oleo," "Doxy," and "Tenor Madness" have become jazz standards. To this day, Rollins's live performances continue to be the stuff that legends are made of.

Musically speaking:

Sonny Rollins is known for his sardonic wit and "thematic improvisation"—his ability to get inside an idea or theme, cull from it, distill its essence, and use it for a series of variations, often forsaking the chord changes to keep the embellishments going. Rollins reacts to the moment, playing off the other musicians, avoiding licks and clichés. The most complex phrases, sustained lines, and dazzling runs are held back until just the right moment—the solo's climax. As he said in an interview with Eric Nisensen for Jazz One magazine, "When I'm really playing at my best, the music is sort of playing itself. I'm just standing there moving the keys. The music is coming out, but I am not thinking about it. That's the state I try to reach."

Rollins came of age during the advent of tape and LP records, which had a large impact on jazz by creating the space for extended solos. He sustains interest during long solo flights by employing one of Thelonious Monk's philosophies: use the melody as more than just a launching pad; use it as a building block for the solo.

Another aspect of Rollins's style is his remarkable sense of rhythm. He establishes a rhythmic shape and then plays with it, moving it in and out of time. Certain notes are lengthened, others are cut short—the rhythm is displaced almost as if he were removing the bar lines. A long flurry of 16th notes could be followed by a stuttering group of 8th notes, punctuated by a stiff staccato bark (meas. B1–5), giving his solos an almost speech-like quality (meas. A17–29). His enormous vocabulary and seemingly endless supply of ideas make Sonny Rollins a giant among jazz musicians.

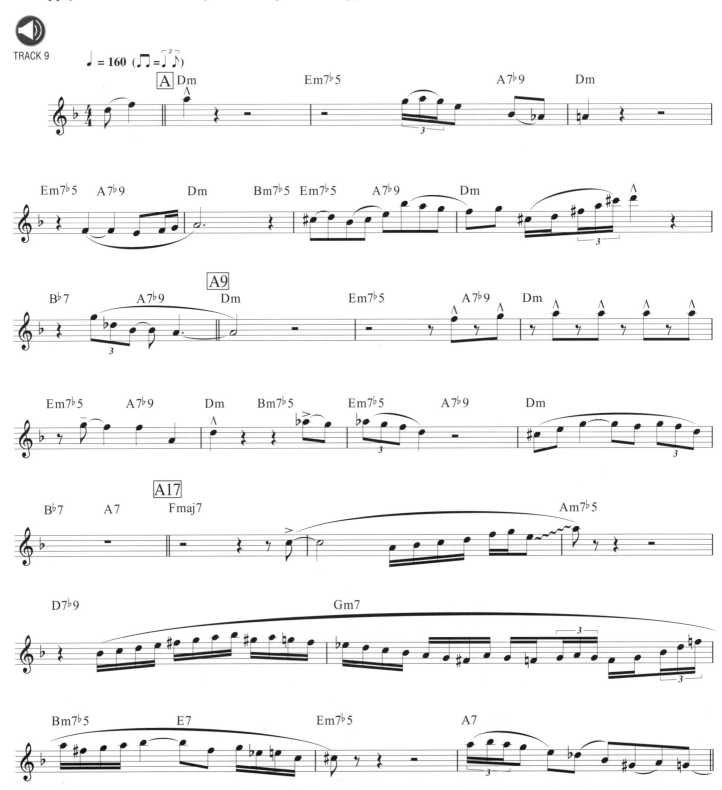

*Play as straight eighth notes.

Sonny Rollins Selected Discography

1956   *Saxophone Colossus* – Original Jazz Classics

1956   *Sonny Rollins Plus 4* (with Clifford Brown) – Original Jazz Classics

1957   *Way Out West* – Original Jazz Classics

1957   *Night At The Village Vanguard*, Vols. I & II (Live) – Blue Note

1962   *The Bridge* – Bluebird/RCA

1972   *Sonny Rollins' Next Album* – Milestone

1996   *Sonny Rollins Plus Three* – Milestone

Hank Mobley seen here with Art Blakey. Mobley was the torch-bearer of the hard bop movement of the 1960s.

HANK MOBLEY

(1930 – 1986)

Equal parts blues, funk, and bop, tenor saxophonist Hank Mobley typified the hard bop movement of the 1960s.

Born in Georgia and raised in Elizabeth, NJ, Mobley first played piano, then picked up the saxophone at age 16. He got his start as a member of the house band in a Newark, NJ nightclub, where he backed stars like Miles Davis, Dexter Gordon, and Bud Powell. In 1951, drummer Max Roach hired Mobley for his band. After two years he left to join Dizzy Gillespie's band, participating in four recording sessions with Diz. From 1954–56, Mobley was an original member of Art Blakey and Horace Silver's Jazz Messengers. When Silver split off to form his own group in 1956, Mobley went with him.

He then returned briefly to Blakey's Jazz Messengers in 1959. In 1961 he joined Miles Davis's quintet for a short stint, during which he recorded four albums with the group.

Mobley is probably best known for his consistently high-quality recordings and his strong original compositions—twenty-five albums recorded over a fifteen-year period (1955–70)—that helped define the Blue Note label's hard bop sound of the sixties. Mobley spent much of the late sixties in Europe, returning to the U.S. in 1970 to co-lead a quintet with pianist Cedar Walton. By the mid-seventies, bad health had forced his retirement. Blue Note didn't release several of his best recordings until the CD reissues of the mid-eighties.

Musically speaking:

Hank Mobley credited the influence of Coltrane and Davis for the symmetry and contour of his long-flowing lines: a long phrase is answered by a short phrase; an upward moving line is countered by a downward swoop. His playing featured a round tone, with a fertile melodic imagination. His music was full of rhythmically subtle phrases and intricate patterns weaving themselves through the chord changes. When he returned to Blue Note after his association with Davis, his tone had a harder edge and a more aggressive attack.

Throughout his career, Mobley stood in the shadow of saxophone giants Coltrane and Rollins, never fully getting his due during his lifetime—despite his fiery improvisations and his catalog of superb original compositions.

TRACK 10

*Play as straight eighth notes.

Hank Mobley Selected Discography

1957   Hank Mobley and His All-Stars – Blue Note

1958   *Peckin' Time* – Blue Note

1960   *Soul Station* – Blue Note

1961   *Workout* – Blue Note

1963   *No Room for Squares* – Blue Note

1965   *Dippin'* – Blue Note

Harold Land was an inventive soloist whose approach continued to evolve from bebop to modal.

HAROLD LAND

(1928 – 2001)

A fixture of the Los Angeles jazz scene for nearly fifty years, Harold Land's saxophone and flute playing ran the gamut from fiery post-bop solos to sixties-style modal excursions.

Harold Land moved from Houston to San Diego at age five. At sixteen, after hearing Coleman Hawkins's version of "Body and Soul," he took up the saxophone. His first recording was for Savoy in 1949, and the tracks were issued later on the double LP *Black California*. In the early fifties Land moved to L.A., where he met Clifford Brown at a jam session in Eric Dolphy's garage. This led to a two-year tenure with Brown and Max Roach, during which some of Land's finest performances of scintillating bebop were recorded for Emercy Records.

Tired of the road, Land quit the Brown/Roach quintet and settled back in L.A., playing for the next few years (1956–58) with bassist Curtis Counce. Land made his debut as a leader in 1958, and in 1959 he made the critically acclaimed recording *The Fox*. Over the ensuing years, he recorded with Thelonious Monk, Hampton Hawes, Shorty Rodgers, Red Mitchell, and Gerald Wilson. In 1967, Land formed a band with vibraphonist Bobby Hutcherson, beginning a long association that would last the rest of his career. During the seventies, Land co-led a group with Blue Mitchell. In the eighties he toured with the Timeless Allstars, which featured Hutcherson, Cedar Walton, Curtis Fuller, Billy Higgins, and Buster Williams.

Land was a big supporter of the L.A. jazz scene, teaching informally at local high schools and the Jazz Studies program at UCLA.

Musically Speaking:

Land was a creative soloist whose playing continued to evolve over the years, incorporating new and modern ideas and harmonies. Influenced by Coleman Hawkins, Wardell Gray, Lucky Thompson, and John Coltrane, Land was an expressive, solid bebopper. He possessed a focused, dry tone with a soft attack that became edgier as Coltrane's influence on the saxophone grew.

In the following example of Land's bebop style of playing, the melodic approach makes liberal use of arpeggios. In fact, the first two measures are exclusively chord tones. In the first chorus, there is repeated use of the notes G#, A, and G# in a triplet rhythm on the third beat (measures 14, 22, 25, and 30). What makes this interesting is the way Land spanned a variety of harmonic contexts—playing the same notes over different chords (measure 14 is a C7 chord, 22 is an E♭7 chord, and 25 is a B♭7). As per the bebop style, chromatic passing tones are used generously throughout the solo. Also, note the double chromatic approach: surrounding a target note—usually a chord tone—by playing the notes a half step above and a half step below, then landing on the targeted note. This technique is used in measures A6, A10, A31, and B14.

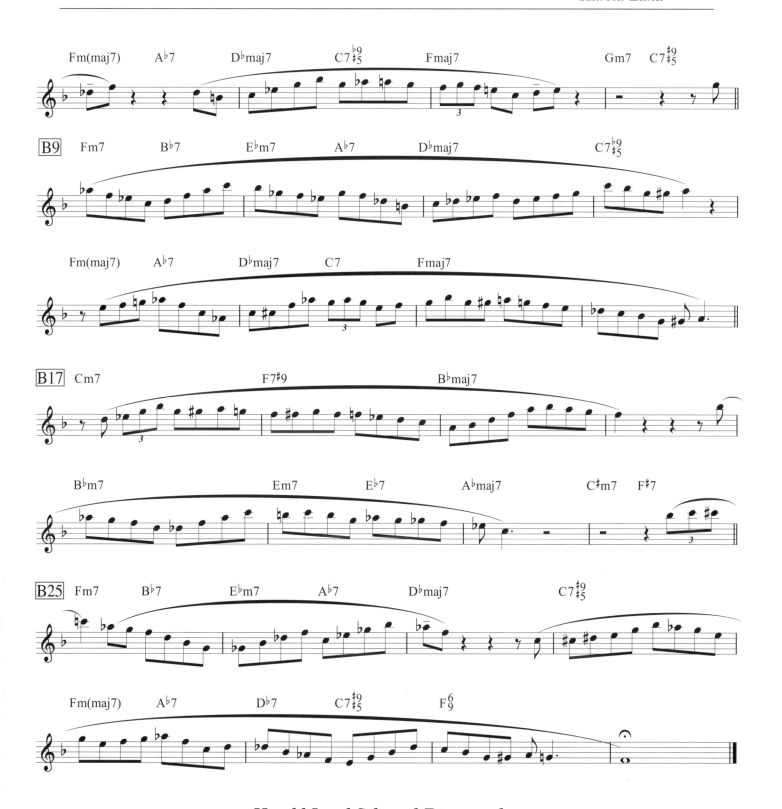

Harold Land Selected Discography

1958 / 1988   *Harold in the Land of Jazz* – Original Jazz Classics

1959 / 1988   *The Fox* – Original Jazz Classics

1960 / 1996   *West Coast Blues* – Original Jazz Classics

1960 / 1990   *Eastward Ho* – Original Jazz Classics

1967   *Total Eclipse* (with Bobby Hutcherson) – Blue Note

1977 / 1990   *Mapenzi* – Concord

STAN GETZ

(1927 – 1991)

Stan Getz enjoyed a long and prolific musical career—nearly half a century. His soloing style was very accessible and his strong lyrical sense made him a favorite among jazz fans.

Born in Philadelphia, PA and raised in New York City, Getz began playing professionally at age fifteen, and made his recording debut a year later with trombonist Jack Teagarden. By the time he was twenty, he had begun honing his craft in the sax sections of some of the major swing bands of the time: Stan Kenton (1944–45); Tommy Dorsey (1945); and Benny Goodman (1945–46). He had his first session as a bandleader in 1946. It was during his stay with Woody Herman's Second Herd (1947–49) that he began to get national attention, being part of the original "Four Brothers" sax section along with Zoot Sims, Herbie Steward, and Serge Chaloff. Getz was also showcased on an ethereal, eight-measure solo on the ballad "Early Autumn," which featured his featherweight, vibrato-free tone.

After leaving Herman, Getz began to lead his own bands. In 1951 he toured Sweden with guitarist Jimmy Raney, playing a new and exciting brand of jazz that was built on energetic interplay on up-tempo tunes and a tonal blend that was a harbinger of the West Coast jazz movement.

Getz's career was derailed by drug problems in the mid-fifties, but back on track by the next decade. In 1958 he moved to Denmark, where he played with other expatriates including Oscar Pettiford and Kenny Clark. Three years later he returned to NYC, where he recorded his personal favorite album Focus, backed by Eddie Sauter's lush arrangements and studio orchestra. His popularity exploded when he joined Charlie Byrd to record the groundbreaking *Jazz Samba* (1962). The tune "Desafinado" became a big hit, and the bossa nova craze, a blend of jazz and Brazilian rhythms, swept the U.S. Getz rode the wave for the next two years, and his collaboration with João Gilberto and Antonio Carlos Jobim crested with the tune "The Girl From Ipanema" (sung by Gilberto, who had never sung professionally until then). The song became one of the best-selling jazz records of all time.

Getz spent the next few years trying to distance himself from the bossa nova craze and returned to playing more challenging jazz. He had an ear for talent, and helped launch the careers of several promising jazz musicians—including Horace Silver, Gary Burton, Chick Corea, and Joanne Brackeen. In 1971, Getz formed a quartet with pianist Corea, bassist Stanley Clarke, drummer Tony Williams, and percussionist Airto Moreira. Getz made a couple more memorable jazz recordings during the seventies, and spent the latter part of the decade exploring fusion. By the 1980s he was back recording straight-ahead jazz albums and teaching at Stanford University. He continued to tour and record up until his death in 1991. His final album, *People Time* (recorded three months before his death), was a masterful set of duets featuring pianist Kenny Barron.

Musically speaking:

Stan Getz was a paramount stylist of the tenor sax. He was known as "the Sound" due to his light but expansive tone and slow vibrato. His first major influence was Lester Young; this can be heard in Getz's tone and linear approach. As time wore on, his tone became broader with a slightly more forceful attack. For the most part, he shunned electronics (except during his brief foray into fusion), preferring to play acoustically to fill concert halls with his pure, natural tone. Never content to rest on his many accolades, Getz was constantly exploring new musical territory. What remained constant, however, was the romantic and lyrical quality of his improvisations.

Another key element of Getz's style, as demonstrated in the following example, was the "theme and variations" approach—creating a series of variations on the original germ of a melodic idea. One way he did this was by displacing phrases, or starting a repeated phrase at a different point in the measure (as in measures A1–7, C9–13, and throughout section D).

Getz was also a master of sequencing motifs, as in measures A24–27, B1–2, and B17–20. (The notes marked "PK" are to be played with the palm keys.) From the breakneck tempos of his hard-swinging material, to the tender romanticism of his ballad style, Getz's playing was consistently compelling.

Stan Getz was a very lyrical player whose phrasing owed a big debt to Lester Young.

Stan Getz Selected Discography

1951–53	*The Complete Recordings of the Stan Getz Quintet with Jimmy Raney* – Mosaic
1961	*Focus* – Verve
1962	*Jazz Samba* – Verve
1963	*Getz/Gilberto* – Verve
1972	*Captain Marvel* – Columbia
1975	*The Peacocks* – Columbia
1982	*Pure Getz* – Concord

*Charlie Rouse's restrained melodic style was the perfect
compliment to Thelonious Monk's angular playing.*

CHARLIE ROUSE

(1924 – 1988)

Best known for his long association with Thelonious Monk (1959–1970), Charlie Rouse's smooth bebop-style tenor was a perfect foil to Monk's choppy, angular playing.

Charlie Rouse's early career found him playing with the Billy Eckstine (1944) and Dizzy Gillespie (1945) big bands. Rouse made his recording debut in 1947 with Tadd Dameron and Fats Navarro. In 1949 he was hired to replace his idol, Ben Webster, in the Ellington orchestra; he appears in the 1950 Universal short film *Salute To Duke Ellington*. Rouse lost the Ellington gig when a lost birth certificate denied him a passport for a European tour. He then played for a time with the Basie octet (1950), participated in Clifford Brown's first recording session (1953), and played with the Oscar Pettiford Sextet (1955). In 1956, Rouse formed the hard bop quintet Les Jazz Modes with French horn player Julius Watkins. Sonny Rollins recommended Rouse to Monk, with whom he began his long-term tenure in 1959. A brilliant and demanding bandleader, Monk was known for rarely doing a second take in the studio, for fear of losing the spontaneity of the performance. Rouse's ability to handle the harmonically complex compositions of Monk on the first take was demonstrated on the group's many essential sides recorded for Riverside and Columbia (1961–68).

Rouse would occasionally lead recording dates for Blue Note and Epic during the 1960s. In the eighties he co-led the band Sphere, which continued to explore Monk's music. His final three recording projects served to demonstrate his close connection to Monk: 1984's duet with soprano saxophonist Steve Lacy, *Ask Me Now* (a tribute collection of Monk's music produced by Hal Willner); 1988's classic recording *Carmen Sings Monk* with Carmen McRae; and Rouse's final project, a birthday salute to Monk called Epistrophy, recorded just weeks before his death.

Musically Speaking:

Charlie Rouse's playing was bop influenced, although never "notey." He soloed with restraint and was patient and deliberate in his phrasing. Rouse never strayed too far from the melody; he would often restate the melody at the outset of his solo to set up his own improvisations. Also a fine ballad player, Rouse had a warm, breathy attack à la Ben Webster. He took his time, playing thoughtful, lyrical melodies.

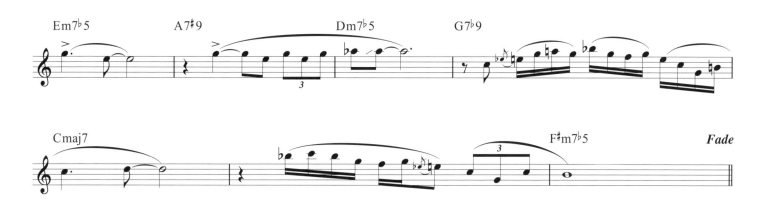

Charlie Rouse Selected Discography

1960   *Taking Care of Business* – Jazzland

1977   *Moment's Notice* – Storyville

With Thelonious Monk:

1962   *Monk's Dream* – Columbia

1963   *Criss-Cross* – Columbia

1966   *Straight, No Chaser* – Columbia

1967   *Underground* – Columbia

With Sphere:

1982   *Four in One* – Elektra

JOHN COLTRANE ("TRANE")

(1926 – 1967)

John Coltrane was a remarkable innovator and one of the most influential jazz musicians of the second half of the Twentieth Century.

Born in Hamlet, NC, the son of a tailor and part-time violinist, Coltrane started out playing clarinet, and at age fifteen switched to alto saxophone. From 1945–46 he played alto in a Navy band based in Hawaii. Upon discharge, he moved to Philadelphia (where his family had relocated), and there played with King Kolax and Joe Webb. In 1947 he picked up the tenor to join alto saxophonist Eddie "Cleanhead" Vinson's band (the alto chair was already filled by Vinson). He was then enlisted by Dizzy Gillespie to play in his big band (1948–49) and later his sextet (1950–51). It was with Gillespie that Coltrane made his recording debut. That was followed by gigs with R&B saxophonist Earl Bostic (1952), saxophonist Johnny Hodges (1953–54), and a short stint with organist Jimmy Smith (1955).

Coltrane gained national prominence when he joined Miles Davis's group in late 1955. Critics were hard on the young tenor player whose tone was considered "too edgy" and whose harmonic sense extended beyond his technique—but under Miles's tutelage, Coltrane's playing improved rapidly. He practiced obsessively, woodshedding during the day, then practicing between sets at gigs, wherever he could—backstage, in the kitchen, in the alley, and even on stage. His performances on Davis's classic recordings for Prestige and Columbia (1955–61) were instrumental in making him an international star. By 1956, Coltrane and Sonny Rollins were considered the top young tenor players of the time; they even battled

© Lee Tanner

John Coltrane altered the sound of jazz with his system of re-harmonization and tonal explorations. His influence is far-reaching.

to a "draw" on Rollins's classic blues "Tenor Madness"—the only time they ever recorded together. Prestige also signed Coltrane as a leader on many of their "blowing session" albums.

Davis fired Coltrane in early 1957, because his heroin habit had made him unreliable. Trane returned to Philadelphia, kicked the habit, and underwent a spiritual awakening. He returned to NYC in the summer of 1957 to work with Thelonious Monk, who had a regular gig at the Five Spot Cafe. Their association raised Monk's profile and allowed Coltrane to absorb Monk's harmonic knowledge. Trane's playing grew more adventurous and took bebop-styled improvisation to another level by charging through the chords very aggressively, cramming in long runs at mach speed (described by critic Ira Gitler as "sheets of sound"). That same year, Coltrane made his recording debut as a leader on *Blue Train* (Blue Note Records). By the time he returned to Miles Davis's band in 1958, he was considered the most important tenor player of his day.

While on his second tour of duty with Davis, Coltrane participated in two classic recordings— *Milestones* (1958) and *Kind Of Blue* (1959). His solo career overlapped his days with Miles; his first effort for the Atlantic was the landmark *Giant Steps*, featuring all original compositions. The recording showcased his new harmonic approach with complex chord substitutions dubbed "Coltrane changes." No longer just a great player, Coltrane was now admired as a great innovator.

In 1960, Coltrane struck out on his own to form his own quartet. He hired pianist McCoy Tyner, drummer Elvin Jones, and tried several bassists before settling on Jimmy Garrison in 1961. The music started to move in a new direction, getting away from the complex chord progressions and into compositions utilizing one- or two-chord vamps and modes. He also reintroduced the soprano sax, an instrument that hadn't been heard since the 1920s. Coltrane's new voice and modal approach was applied to the show tune "My Favorite Things," which became a staple of his live shows. In 1961, Coltrane became the first artist signed to the new Impulse! Label, which gave him complete artistic control. He added saxophonist Eric Dolphy to his group, pushing the music in a more avant-garde direction. Late in 1961, Trane recorded over a period of five nights at NYC's Village Vanguard. The resulting *Live at the Village Vanguard* featured intense, extended, adventuresome solos. While with Impulse!, Coltrane took major musical risks. His interest in world music and eastern spirituality culminated in 1964's *A Love Supreme*—a four-part suite based on simple, haunting melodies. Influenced further by the most radical of saxophonists (Albert Ayler, Archie Shepp, and Pharaoh Sanders), he began to drop the melodies and explore free improvisation and sound explorations, i.e. multi-phonics, overtones, and altissimo register (1965's *Ascension*). He often expanded his quartet with other saxophonists, trumpets, percussion, and even a second bass player. By 1966, the original group had disbanded and was replaced by his wife Alice Coltrane on piano, Pharaoh Sanders on saxophone, Rashied Ali on drums, and Jimmy Garrison still on bass. Following their successful tour of Japan, Coltrane's health rapidly declined. He died July 17, 1967 at age 40.

Musically Speaking:

Coltrane's playing can be divided into three overlapping periods, each one lasting roughly three years. The first, "Sheets of Sound" (1957–60), is characterized by compositions with lots of chord changes, or simple compositions that he made complex by his system of re-harmonization. Where Coleman Hawkins had perfected a method of sounding every chord, Coltrane expanded that by attempting to play all the notes in every chord in rapid-fire succession. In order to play the entire scale and its alterations to any chord, he rearranged his rhythmic approach, changing the basic unit of the jazz solo from eighth notes to sixteenth notes. Uneven or asymmetrical phrases, including seven-, nine-, and eleven-note groupings, quickly became the norm. A Coltrane solo from this period was bursting with virtuosity.

Having pushed jazz harmonies about as far as they could go, Coltrane set out on a different path—his "Modal" period (1960–64). He reduced the harmonic challenges to a minimum, basing his compositions and improvisations on simple one- or two-chord vamps and modes. The soloist was now allowed to play on one chord or scale for sixteen measures or longer. Solos from this period were typified by long improvisations—sometimes forty-five minutes in length! These excursions were filled with complex, arrhythmic runs and phrases using a wide array of scales and modes—Pentatonic, Indian, Oriental, etc. The lack of harmonic movement influenced a change from vertical to horizontal thinking. Coltrane chose to explore the extreme registers of the saxophone, punctuating statements with low honks or high, emotive cries. He began to change the role of the rhythm section in jazz by employing unorthodox use of space, implied pedal points, and a relentless drive. The rhythm section could no longer play just an accompaniment role; the whole quartet contributed equally to the final result.

The final stage, from 1964–67, found Coltrane exploring on many new levels. He began to expand the tonal palate and emotional scope of the saxophone by using multiphonics (playing two or more notes simultaneously) and alternate fingerings to change the instrument's sonorities. He also changed the size and instrumentation of his groups so that he could explore textures, structures, and forms. He again explored harmony, this time the structural concept of pantonality (in which all the notes become one tonality, no longer a series of keys or modes). Coltrane could now play in a "free" context with no preconceived structures or forms. On his last recording, he was accompanied only by drummer Rashied Ali.

The following example is a solo in the style of Coltrane's "Sheets of Sound" period.

TRACK 14

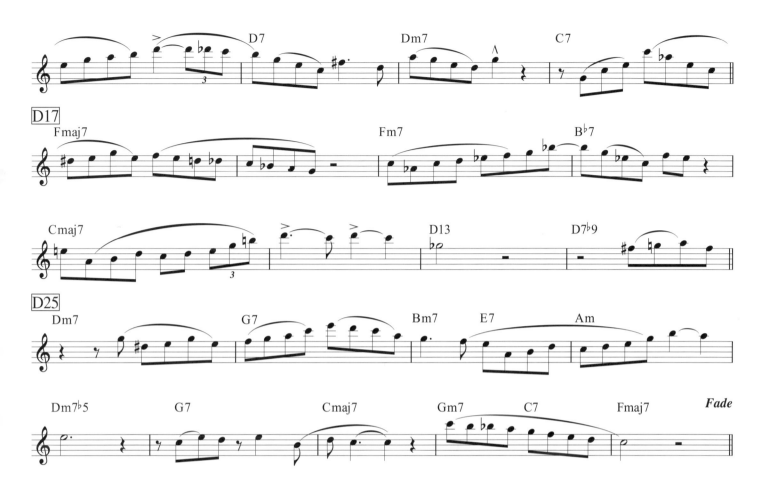

John Coltrane Selected Discography

1957   *Blue Train* – Blue Note

1959   *Giant Steps* – Atlantic

1960   *My Favorite Things* – Atlantic

1961   *Complete Africa/Brass Sessions* – Impulse!

1961   *Live at the Village Vanguard* – Impulse!

1963   *John Coltrane and Johnny Hartman* – Impulse!

1963   *Live at Birdland* – Impulse!

1964   *Crescent* – Impulse!

1964   *A Love Supreme* – Impulse!

1965   *Meditations* – Impulse!

Joe Henderson's understated and introverted style set him apart from his contemporaries.

JOE HENDERSON

(1937 – 2001)

Joe Henderson was able to walk the tightrope between the mainstream players of the 1960s and the new direction of the avant-garde.

Born in Lima, OH, one of fifteen children, Henderson was encouraged by his parents to study music. He began as a student at Kentucky State College, then moved to Detroit and studied with sax instructor Larry Teal at the Teal School of Music. In addition to learning the finer points of saxophone playing, he was introduced to harmony and theory. He then enrolled in Wayne State University, where he played with classmates Yusef Lateef (sax), Barry Harris (piano), and Donald Byrd (trumpet).

After a two-year hitch in the army (1960–62), Henderson moved to New York City. Soon after arriving, he made his recording debut with Kenny Dorham on a date for Blue Note. From 1964–66 he was a member of Horace Silver's quintet. He then resumed freelancing and appeared on nearly thirty recordings for Blue Note, playing on sessions that ran the gamut from hard bop to avant-garde. For a brief period in 1967, he joined Miles Davis's classic quintet featuring Herbie Hancock, Tony Williams, and Ron Carter. In 1967–68, Henderson co-led a band with Freddie Hubbard called the Jazz Communicators, and from 1969–70 he was reunited with Herbie Hancock in Hancock's funk-leaning sextet. Henderson recorded twelve albums for the Milestone label (1967–76) that ranged from hard bop, to modal excursions, to fusion and seventies funk. During this time he also recorded many of his own socio-politically-inspired compositions, including "Power to the People," "In Search of Blackness," and "Black Narcissus."

In 1971, Henderson briefly joined the jazz/rock band Blood, Sweat and Tears. After BST he moved to San Francisco, where he continued to perform and record. By the 1980s he was leading his own outfit and focusing more on his compositions, exploring form, structure, and textures. His career really took off in the nineties, thanks to a series of albums for Verve. Each of the three recordings was a tribute to a different artist: Billy Strayhorn, Miles Davis, and Antonio Carlos Jobim (see the discography for titles). After thirty years, Henderson finally got his recognition as a major player on the jazz sax scene. He made his final recording in 1997 and continued to tour until his death in 2001.

Musically speaking:

Jazz journalist Gary Giddens described Joe Henderson's sound as "a bewitching tone that can be both gruff and tender, virile and hollow in the space of a phrase." Henderson had a unique voice that set him apart from the dominant jazz sounds of the sixties: Coltrane and Rollins. While Trane's and Rollins's styles were very aggressive and extroverted, Henderson's playing was more introverted and vulnerable. Probing themes with fragmented phrases and a sense of mystery, his solos were marked by long lines that floated in and out of rhythm like a modern Lester Young. Henderson's flute-like sonorities in the upper register were an important part of his distinctive sound.

Henderson claimed Stan Getz and Charlie Parker as early influences, but his style does not bear the identifiable stamp of any one player. One of the interesting facets of his style was his ability to adapt to the musical situation, thus giving him many identities. Because of his chameleonic traits, there seems to be no recognizable heir to his lineage—although he has influenced countless saxophonists.

In the following example of Henderson's style, notice how the simple melodic approach is coupled with rhythmic variety. The approach keeps mostly diatonic to the modal and tonal centers of the tune, demonstrating that it's not necessary to be chromatically complex to be effective.

Joe Henderson Selected Discography

1963	*Our Thing* – Blue Note
1964	*In 'n Out* – Blue Note
1964	*Inner Urge* – Blue Note
1966	*Mode for Joe* – Blue Note
1967	*The Kicker* – Original Jazz Classics
1991	*Lush Life: The Music of Billy Strayhorn* – Verve
1992	*So Near, So Far (Musings for Miles)* – Verve
1994	*Double Rainbow: The Music of Antonio Carlos Jobim* – Verve

George Coleman's virtuosity is exhibited in his remarkable technique and inventive harmonic style.

GEORGE COLEMAN

(1935 –)

Influenced by the rich Memphis culture of blues, R&B, and jazz, George Coleman is a masterful tenor player with an aggressive, muscular style. He sadly remains grossly under-recorded and underappreciated.

Largely self-taught, Memphis, TN-born George Coleman picked up the saxophone at age fifteen. Two years later in 1952, he started working with B.B. King's band (and did again in 1955–56). In 1957 Coleman moved to Chicago, where he played with Walter Perkins' group MJT+3. In 1958 he relocated to New York City and was soon playing with the Max Roach quartet (1958–59), the Slide Hampton octet (1959–61), and Wild Bill Davis (1962). The big break came when John Coltrane recommended Coleman to Miles Davis as his own replacement in the quintet—playing alongside Herbie Hancock, Ron Carter, and Tony Williams (1963–64). Coleman recorded four albums with Miles during his tenure with the band.

After leaving Davis's band, Coleman worked with Lionel Hampton, Elvin Jones, Chet Baker, and Charles McPherson. Since that time he has led his own groups (his first recording as a leader was in 1977) and been featured as a sideman on various projects, including Herbie Hancock's classic recording *Maiden Voyage*.

Musically speaking:

George Coleman was first influenced by Charlie Parker, Sonny Stitt, Sonny Rollins, and later John Coltrane. He is an inventive, harmonic stylist whose playing has a melodic intensity. His playing is daring; he's willing to take chances. His virtuosity is dazzling, featuring rapid, cascading, spiraling lines. His music is expressive and conversational. He moves swiftly through the changes, often using chord substitutions and shifting harmonies to foreshadow the changes. He intersperses his jazz lines with references to his blues roots. Coleman has a great ear, remarkable technique, and a broad penetrating tone quality. He uses the entire range of the horn to great dramatic effect.

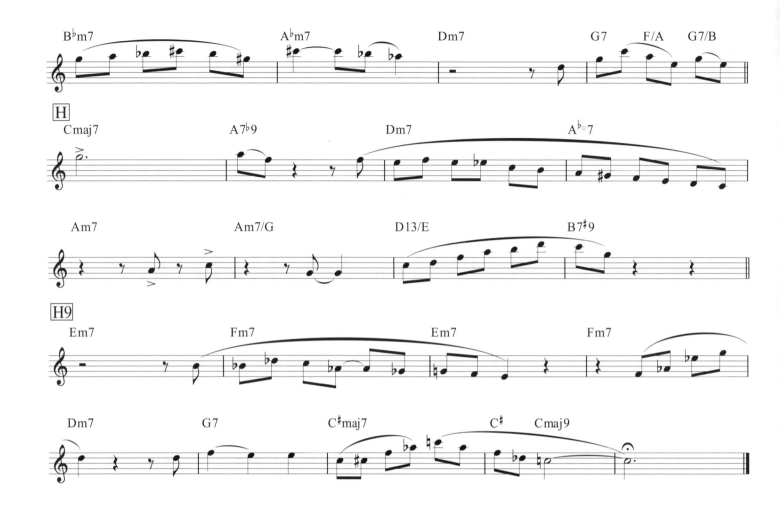

George Coleman Selected Discography

1985   *Manhattan Panorama* – Evidence

1987   *At Yoshi's* – Evidence

1991   *My Horns of Plenty* – Verve

With Miles Davis:

1963   *Seven Steps to Heaven* – Columbia

1964   *My Funny Valentine* – Columbia

1964   *Four & More* – Columbia

With Herbie Hancock:

1965   *Maiden Voyage* – Blue Note

BIBLIOGRAPHY

BOOKS

Balliett, Whitney: *Collected Works: A Journal of Jazz, 1954–2000* – St. Martin's Press.

Balliett, Whitney: *Goodbyes and Other Messages: A Journal of Jazz, 1981-1990* – Oxford Press.

Berliner, Paul: *Thinking in Jazz: The Infinite Art of Improvisation* – University of Chicago Press.

Cole, Bill: *John Coltrane* – Schirmer Books.

Dance, Stanley: *The World of Count Basie* – Da Capo Press.

Dance, Stanley: *The World of Duke Ellington* – Scribner's Sons.

Davis, Miles with Quincy Troupe: *Miles, the Autobiography* – Simon & Schuster, Inc.

Erlewine, Michael and Vladimir Bogdaov, Chris Woodstra, Scott Yanow, eds.:
    All Music Guide To Jazz – Miller Freeman Books.

Giddins, Gary: *Visions of Jazz: The First Century* – Oxford Press.

Kirchner, Bill, ed.: *A Miles Davis Reader* – Smithsonian Institute Press.

Porter, Lewis: *Lester Young* – Twayne Publishers.

Taylor, Arthur: *Notes and Tones: Musician to Musician Interviews* – A Perigee Book.

Thomas, J. C.: *Chasin' the Trane* – Da Capo Press

Ullman, Michael: *Jazz Lives: Portraits in Words and Pictures* – New Republic Books.

Williams, Martin: *The Jazz Tradition* – Oxford University Press.

ARTICLES

Balliett, Whitney: "Big Ben." *The New Yorker*, August 20–27, 2001.

Barrett, John R. Jr.: "Joe Henderson." *Jazz Improv*, Vol. 4 No. 2.

Belden, Bob: "Sonny Rollins The Man." *DownBeat*, August 1997.

Heckman, Don: "Prez and Hawk, Saxophone Fountainheads." *DownBeat*, January 1963.

Nemeyer, Eric: "George Coleman, the Tenor of Authority—An Interview with Jazz Improv."
    Jazz Improv, Vol. 3, No. 4.

Nisenson, Eric: "Sonny Rollins Is in the House." *Jazz One*, April 1999.

ABOUT THE AUTHOR

Two-time (1999 and 2000) Nashville Music Awards nominee for "Miscellaneous Wind Instrumentalist of the Year", saxophonist Dennis Taylor (tenor, alto, soprano, and baritone) has been playing the sax professionally for more than twenty-five years. He's toured and/or recorded with a wide variety of artists including Clarence "Gatemouth" Brown, Buckwheat Zydeco, Duke Robillard, Shelby Lynne, Eddy "The Chief" Clearwater, Robert Jr. Lockwood, "Mighty" Sam McClain, Sam Moore (Sam & Dave), Dan Penn, Jay McShann, Kenny Rogers, and John Hammond. Taylor has played on five Grammy-nominated albums. He has appeared on "Austin City Limits," "The Road," "Country Music Hall of Fame 25th Anniversary Celebration," "Texas Connection," "ABC in Concert Country," "American Music Shop," and "Music City Tonight."

This is Taylor's third saxophone book for Hal Leonard Corporation; his previous titles are *Blues Saxophone: An In-Depth Look at the Styles of the Masters* and *Amazing Phrasing Saxophone: Fifty Ways to Improve Your Improvisational Skills*.

ARTIST TRANSCRIPTIONS®

Artist Transcriptions are authentic, note-for-note transcriptions of the hottest artists in jazz, pop, and rock today. These outstanding, accurate arrangements are in an easy-to-read format which includes all essential lines. Artist Transcriptions can be used to perform, sequence or reference.

GUITAR & BASS

The Guitar Style of George Benson
00660113 ....$14.95

The Guitar Book of Pierre Bensusan
00699072 ....$19.95

Ron Carter – Acoustic Bass
00672331 ....$16.95

Stanley Clarke Collection
00672307 ....$19.95

Al Di Meola – Cielo E Terra
00604041 ....$14.95

Al Di Meola – Friday Night in San Francisco
00660115 ....$14.95

Al Di Meola – Music, Words, Pictures
00604043 ....$14.95

Kevin Eubanks Guitar Collection
00672319 ....$19.95

The Jazz Style of Tal Farlow
00673245 ....$19.95

Bela Fleck and the Flecktones
00672359 Melody/Lyrics/Chords $18.95

David Friesen – Years Through Time
00673253 ....$14.95

Best of Frank Gambale
00672336 ....$22.95

Jim Hall – Jazz Guitar Environments
00699389 Book/CD $19.95

Jim Hall – Exploring Jazz Guitar
00699306 ....$17.95

Allan Holdsworth – Reaching for the Uncommon Chord
00604049 ....$14.95

Leo Kottke – Eight Songs
00699215 ....$14.95

Wes Montgomery – Guitar Transcriptions
00675536 ....$17.95

Joe Pass Collection
00672353 ....$18.95

John Patitucci
00673216 ....$14.95

Django Reinhardt Anthology
00027083 ....$14.95

The Genius of Django Reinhardt
00026711 ....$10.95

Django Reinhardt – A Treasury of Songs
00026715 ....$12.95

Johnny Smith Guitar Solos
00672374 ....$16.95

Mike Stern Guitar Book
00673224 ....$16.95

Mark Whitfield
00672320 ....$19.95

Jack Wilkins – Windows
00673249 ....$14.95

Gary Willis Collection
00672337 ....$19.95

SAXOPHONE

Julian "Cannonball" Adderly Collection
00673244 ....$19.95

Michael Brecker
00673237 ....$19.95

Michael Brecker Collection
00672429 ....$19.95

The Brecker Brothers... And All Their Jazz
00672351 ....$19.95

Best of the Brecker Brothers
00672447 ....$19.95

Benny Carter Plays Standards
00672315 ....$22.95

Benny Carter Collection
00672314 ....$22.95

James Carter Collection
00672394 ....$19.95

John Coltrane – Giant Steps
00672349 ....$19.95

John Coltrane – A Love Supreme
00672494 ....$12.95

John Coltrane Plays "Coltrane Changes"
00672493 ....$19.95

Coltrane Plays Standards
00672453 ....$19.95

John Coltrane Solos
00673233 ....$22.95

Paul Desmond Collection
00672328 ....$19.95

Paul Desmond – Standard Time
00672454 ....$19.95

Stan Getz
00699375 ....$18.95

Stan Getz – Bossa Novas
00672377 ....$19.95

Stan Getz – Standards
00672375 ....$17.95

The Coleman Hawkins Collection
00672523 ....$19.95

Joe Henderson – Selections from "Lush Life" & "So Near So Far"
00673252 ....$19.95

Best of Joe Henderson
00672330 ....$22.95

Best of Kenny G
00673239 ....$19.95

Kenny G – Breathless
00673229 ....$19.95

Kenny G – Classics in the Key of G
00672462 ....$19.95

Kenny G – Faith: A Holiday Album
00672485 ....$14.95

Kenny G – The Moment
00672373 ....$19.95

Kenny G – Paradise
00672516 ....$14.95

Joe Lovano Collection
00672326 ....$19.95

James Moody Collection – Sax and Flute
00672372 ....$19.95

The Frank Morgan Collection
00672416 ....$19.95

The Art Pepper Collection
00672301 ....$19.95

Sonny Rollins Collection
00672444 ....$19.95

David Sanborn Collection
00675000 ....$16.95

The Lew Tabackin Collection
00672455 ....$19.95

Stanley Turrentine Collection
00672334 ....$19.95

Ernie Watts Saxophone Collection
00673256 ....$18.95

PIANO & KEYBOARD

Monty Alexander Collection
00672338 ....$19.95

Monty Alexander Plays Standards
00672487 ....$19.95

Kenny Barron Collection
00672318 ....$22.95

The Count Basie Collection
00672520 ....$19.95

Warren Bernhardt Collection
00672364 ....$19.95

Cyrus Chesnut Collection
00672439 ....$19.95

Billy Childs Collection
00673242 ....$19.95

Chick Corea – Elektric Band
00603126 ....$15.95

Chick Corea – Paint the World
00672300 ....$12.95

Bill Evans Collection
00672365 ....$19.95

Bill Evans – Piano Interpretations
00672425 ....$19.95

The Bill Evans Trio
00672510 Volume 1: 1959-1961 ......$24.95
00672511 Volume 2: 1962-1965 ......$24.95
00672512 Volume 3: 1968-1974 ......$24.95
00672513 Volume 4: 1979-1980 ......$24.95

The Benny Goodman Collection
00672492 ....$16.95

Benny Green Collection
00672329 ....$19.95

Vince Guaraldi Jazz Transcriptions
00672486 ....$19.95

Herbie Hancock Collection
00672419 ....$19.95

Gene Harris Collection
00672446 ....$19.95

Hampton Hawes
00672438 ....$19.95

Ahmad Jamal Collection
00672322 ....$22.95

Brad Mehldau Collection
00672476 ....$19.95

Thelonious Monk Plays Jazz Standards – Volume 1
00672390 ....$19.95

Thelonious Monk Plays Jazz Standards – Volume 2
00672391 ....$19.95

Thelonious Monk – Intermediate Piano Solos
00672392 ....$14.95

Jelly Roll Morton – The Piano Rolls
00672433 ....$12.95

Michel Petrucciani
00673226 ....$17.95

Bud Powell Classics
00672371 ....$19.95

Bud Powell Collection
00672376 ....$19.95

André Previn Collection
00672437 ....$19.95

Gonzalo Rubalcaba Collection
00672507 ....$19.95

Horace Silver Collection
00672303 ....$19.95

Art Tatum Collection
00672316 ....$22.95

Art Tatum Solo Book
00672355 ....$19.95

Billy Taylor Collection
00672357 ....$24.95

McCoy Tyner
00673215 ....$16.95

Cedar Walton Collection
00672321 ....$19.95

The Teddy Wilson Collection
00672434 ....$19.95

CLARINET

Buddy De Franco Collection
00672423 ....$19.95

TROMBONE

J.J. Johnson Collection
00672332 ....$19.95

FLUTE

Eric Dolphy Collection
00672379 ....$19.95

James Newton – Improvising Flute
00660108 ....$14.95

The Lew Tabackin Collection
00672455 ....$19.95

TRUMPET

The Chet Baker Collection
00672435 ....$19.95

Randy Brecker
00673234 ....$17.95

The Brecker Brothers...And All Their Jazz
00672351 ....$19.95

Best of the Brecker Brothers
00672447 ....$19.95

Miles Davis – Originals Volume 1
00672448 ....$19.95

Miles Davis – Originals Volume 2
00672451 ....$19.95

Miles Davis – Standards Vol. 1
00672450 ....$19.95

Miles Davis – Standards Vol. 2
00672449 ....$19.95

The Dizzy Gillespie Collection
00672479 ....$19.95

Freddie Hubbard
00673214 ....$14.95

Tom Harrell Jazz Trumpet
00672382 ....$19.95

The Chuck Mangione Collection
00672506 ....$19.95

Prices and availability subject to change without notice.
Some products may not be available outside the U.S.A.

For More Information, See Your Local Music Dealer, Or Write To:

HAL•LEONARD® CORPORATION
7777 W. Bluemound Rd. P.O. Box 13819 Milwaukee, WI 53213

Visit our web site for a complete listing of our titles with songlists.
www.halleonard.com

0104

Presenting the Hal Leonard JAZZ PLAY ALONG SERIES

DUKE ELLINGTON Vol. 1 00841644
Caravan • Don't Get Around Much Anymore • In a Mellow Tone • In a Sentimental Mood • It Don't Mean a Thing (If It Ain't Got That Swing) • Perdido • Prelude to a Kiss • Satin Doll • Sophisticated Lady • Take the "A" Train.

MILES DAVIS Vol. 2 00841645
All Blues • Blue in Green • Four • Half Nelson • Milestones • Nardis • Seven Steps to Heaven • So What • Solar • Tune Up.

THE BLUES Vol. 3 00841646
Billie's Bounce (Bill's Bounce) • Birk's Works • Blues for Alice • Blues in the Closet • C-Jam Blues • Freddie Freeloader • Mr. P.C. • Now's the Time • Tenor Madness • Things Ain't What They Used to Be.

JAZZ BALLADS Vol. 4 00841691
Body and Soul • But Beautiful • Here's That Rainy Day • Misty • My Foolish Heart • My Funny Valentine • My One and Only Love • My Romance • The Nearness of You.

THE BEST OF BEBOP Vol. 5 00841689
Anthropology • Donna Lee • Doxy • Epistrophy • Lady Bird • Oleo • Ornithology • Scrapple from the Apple • Woodyn' You • Yardbird Suite.

JAZZ CLASSICS WITH EASY CHANGES Vol. 6 00841690
Blue Train • Comin' Home Baby • Footprints • Impressions • Killler Joe • Moanin' • Sidewinder • St. Thomas • Stolen Moments • Well You Needn't (It's Over Now).

ESSENTIAL JAZZ STANDARDS Vol. 7 00843000
Autumn Leaves • Cotton Tail • Easy Living • I Remember You • If I Should Lose You • Lullaby of Birdland • Out of Nowhere • Stella by Starlight • There Will Never Be Another You • When Sunny Gets Blue.

ANTONIO CARLOS JOBIM AND THE ART OF THE BOSSA NOVA Vol. 8 00843001
The Girl from Ipanema (Garota De Ipanema) • How Insensitive (Insensatez) • Meditation (Meditacao) • Once I Loved (Amor Em Paz) (Love in Peace) • One Note Samba (Samba De Uma Nota So) • Quiet Nights of Quiet Stars (Corcovado) • Slightly out of Tune (Desafinado) • So Danco Samba (Jazz 'N' Samba) • Triste • Wave.

DIZZY GILLESPIE Vol. 9 00843002
Birk's Works • Con Alma • Groovin' High • Manteca • A Night in Tunisia • Salt Peanuts • Shawnuff • Things to Come • Tour De Force • Woodyn' You.

DISNEY CLASSICS Vol. 10 00843003
Alice in Wonderland • Beauty and the Beast • Cruella De Vil • Heigh-Ho • Some Day My Prince Will Come • When You Wish upon a Star • Whistle While You Work • Who's Afraid of the Big Bad Wolf • You've Got a Friend in Me • Zip-a-Dee-Doo-Dah.

RODGERS AND HART FAVORITES Vol. 11 00843004
Bewitched • The Blue Room • Dancing on the Ceiling • Have You Met Miss Jones? • I Could Write a Book • The Lady Is a Tramp • Little Girl Blue • My Romance • There's a Small Hotel • You Are Too Beautiful.

ESSENTIAL JAZZ CLASSICS Vol. 12 00843005
Airegin • Ceora • The Frim Fram Sauce • Israel • Milestones • Nefertiti • Red Clay • Satin Doll • Song for My Father • Take Five.

JOHN COLTRANE Vol. 13 00843006
Blue Train (Blue Trane) • Countdown • Cousin Mary • Equinox • Giant Steps • Impressions • Lazy Bird • Mr. P.C. • Moment's Notice • Naima (Neima).

IRVING BERLIN Vol. 14 00843007
Be Careful, It's My Heart • Blue Skies • Change Partners • Cheek to Cheek • How Deep Is the Ocean (How High Is the Sky) • I've Got My Love to Keep Me Warm • Let's Face the Music and Dance • Steppin' Out with My Baby • They Say It's Wonderful • What'll I Do?

RODGERS & HAMMERSTEIN Vol. 15 00843008
Bali Ha'i • Do I Love You Because You're Beautiful? • Hello Young Lovers • I Have Dreamed • It Might as Well Be Spring • Love, Look Away • My Favorite Things • The Surrey with the Fringe on Top • The Sweetest Sounds • Younger Than Springtime.

COLE PORTER Vol. 16 00843009
All of You • At Long Last • Easy to Love (You'd Be So Easy to Love) • Ev'ry Time We Say Goodbye • I Concentrate on You • I've Got You Under My Skin • In the Still of the Night • It's All Right with Me • It's De-Lovely • You'd Be So Nice to Come Home To.

COUNT BASIE Vol. 17 00843010
All of Me • April in Paris • Blues in Hoss Flat • Cute • Jumpin' at the Woodside • Li'l Darlin' • Moten Swing • One O'Clock Jump • Shiny Stockings • Until I Met You.

HAROLD ARLEN Vol. 18 00843011
Ac•cent•tchu•ate the Positive • Between the Devil and the Deep Blue Sea • Come Rain or Come Shine • If I Only Had a Brain • It's Only a Paper Moon • I've Got the World on a String • My Shining Hour • Over the Rainbow • Stormy Weather • That Old Black Magic.

COOL JAZZ Vol. 19 00843012
Bernie's Tune • Boplicity (Be Bop Lives) • Budo • Conception • Django • Five Brothers • Line for Lyons • Walkin' Shoes • Waltz for Debby • Whisper Not.

RODGERS AND HART CLASSICS Vol. 21 00843014
Falling in Love with Love • Isn't it Romantic? • Manhattan • Mountain Greenery • My Funny Valentine • My Heart Stood Still • This Can't Be Love • Thou Swell • Where or When • You Took Advantage of Me.

WAYNE SHORTER Vol. 22 00843015
Children of the Night • ESP • Footprints • Juju • Mahjong • Nefertiti • Nightdreamer • Speak No Evil • Witch Hunt • Yes and No.

LATIN JAZZ Vol. 23 00843016
Agua De Beber (Water to Drink) • Black Orpheus • Chega De Saudade (No More Blues) • Invitation • Mas Que Nada • So Nice (Summer Samba) • Watch What Happens • and more.

EARLY JAZZ STANDARDS Vol. 24 00843017
After You've Gone • Avalon • Indian Summer • Indiana (Back Home Again in Indiana) • Ja-Da • Limehouse Blues • Paper Doll • Poor Butterfly • Rose Room • St. Louis Blues.

CHRISTMAS JAZZ Vol. 25 00843018
The Christmas Song (Chestnuts Roasting on an Open Fire) • The Christmas Waltz • Frosty the Snow Man • (There's No Place Like) Home for the Holidays • I Heard the Bells on Christmas Day • I'll Be Home for Christmas • Let It Snow! Let It Snow! Let It Snow! • Rudolph the Red-Nosed Reindeer • Silver Bells • Snowfall.

CHARLIE PARKER Vol. 26 00843019
Au Privave • Billie's Bounce (Bill's Bounce) • Confirmation • Donna Lee • Moose the Mooche • My Little Suede Shoes • Now's the Time • Ornithology • Scrapple from the Apple • Yardbird Suite.

GREAT JAZZ STANDARDS Vol. 27 00843020
Fly Me to the Moon (In Other Words) • Girl Talk • How High the Moon • I Can't Get Started with You • It Could Happen to You • Lover • Softly As in a Morning Sunrise • Speak Low • Tangerine • Willow Weep for Me.

BIG BAND ERA Vol. 28 00843021
Air Mail Special • Christopher Columbus • Four Brothers • In the Mood • Intermission Riff • Jersey Bounce • Opus One • Stompin' at the Savoy • A String of Pearls • Tuxedo Junction.

LENNON AND MCCARTNEY Vol. 29 00843022
And I Love Her • Blackbird • Come Together • Eleanor Rigby • The Fool on the Hill • Here, There and Everywhere • Lady Madonna • Let It Be • Ticket to Ride • Yesterday.

BLUES BEST Vol. 30 00843023
Basin Street Blues • Bloomdido • D Natural Blues • Everyday I Have the Blues Again • Happy Go Lucky Local • K.C. Blues • The Swingin' Shepherd Blues • Take the Coltrane • Turnaround • and more.

JAZZ IN THREE Vol. 31 00843024
Bluesette • Gravy Waltz • Jitterbug Waltz • Moon River • Oh, What a Beautiful Mornin' • Tenderly • Tennessee Waltz • West Coast Blues • What the World Needs Now Is Love • Wives and Lovers (Hey, Little Girl).

BEST OF SWING Vol. 32 00843025
Alright, Okay, You Win • Cherokee (Indian Love Song) • I'll Be Seeing You • I've Heard That Song Before • Jump, Jive An' Wail • On the Sunny Side of the Street • Route 66 • Sentimental Journey • What's New? • and more.